RIVER
ELECTRIC
WITH LIGHT

RIVER
ELECTRIC
WITH LIGHT

POEMS

Sarah Wetzel

Red Hen Press | Pasadena, CA

Book layout and design by Selena Trager
Cover image: *Embryo* by Belén Fourcade

Library of Congress Cataloging-in-Publication Data

Wetzel, Sarah.
  [Poems. Selections]
  River electric with light / Sarah Wetzel.—First edition.
    pages ; cm
  ISBN 978-1-59709-286-9 (pbk. : alk. paper)
  I. Title.
  PS3623.E894A6 2015
  811'.6—dc23
                    2015006409

The publication of this book was made possible by A Room of Her Own Foundation's To
the Lighthouse Poetry Publication Prize, awarded in 2013 for the best unpublished poetry
collection by a woman.

The National Endowment for the Arts, the Los Angeles County Arts Commission, the Los
Angeles Department of Cultural Affairs, the Dwight Stuart Youth Fund, the Pasadena
Arts & Culture Commission and the City of Pasadena Cultural Affairs Division, Sony
Pictures Entertainment, and the Ahmanson Foundation partially support Red Hen Press.

First Edition
Published by Red Hen Press
www.redhen.org

ACKNOWLEDGMENTS

Grateful acknowledgment to the editors of the publications where the following poems first appear, at times in earlier forms:

Brink: "Birds of the Old City," "Notes on Dadaism"; *Café Review*: "All the Miracles," "Third Version"; *Fifth Wednesday Journal*: "The American Impulse," "A Worship of Rivers"; *Ilanot Journal*: "Infidelity," "Rack of Lamb"; *New Millennium Writings*: "We Will be Left at Galilee"; *Nimrod International Journal*: "Explaining God to Israeli Children," "Vertigo" (Finalist Nimrod Literary Award); *Stirring*: "The Key," "The Veil" (Nominated for a 2012 Pushcart Prize); *Structo*: "Postcards from Gethsemane"; *Superstition Review*: "A Mirage of Shore," "Near Death Experience," "Reprisal," "Revising Prophesy"; *Voices of Israel*: "Another Year of Sin," "Mercy"; *PoetryNet*: December 2012 Poet of the Month.

Versions and live recordings of "We Will be Left at Galilee," "Near Death Experience," "Vertigo," as well as poems contained in my first book *Bathsheba Transatlantic* can be found at www.fishousepoems.org.

My deepest gratitude to all friends, family, poets, teachers, and strangers on trains who made these poems possible. While there are many people who held my hand through the long birth of this book, I particularly thank Timothy Liu, Marcela Sulak, and Dara Barnat. Their feedback and encouragement were as necessary and sustaining as bread. And lest I forget, I wish to thank The Vermont Studio Center whose gifts of time and three hot meals a day during a critical point in my life allowed me to begin many of the poems in this manuscript.

CONTENTS

[THREE]

[FOUR]

For Danny, all my love

RIVER
ELECTRIC

WITH LIGHT

A WORSHIP OF RIVERS

If I must choose a word for you,
let it be river. Not the river's smoothed banks
that, like skin, give form
to breath and blood, the throb
of twenty trillion red cells wildly
ferrying their burdens.
If I must choose a word for you,
let it be the word
for what flows. Down one river,
a ruined house, down another,
eight empty boats bobbing. Inside a ninth,
there is a girl on her knees, knife
in hand. A kind of river
is running through her.
Because the worship of rivers
is also the worship of a chimney
for smoke, the needle its thread
as it closes the wound, of the wire
for its extra electron.
Because all three are worships
of motion, which is why
I race after rainclouds and trains, the postman
and bicycle messengers. Why I think
wind speaks to me. You,
you don't speak. Yet you take
whatever I throw in. Which is why
I will always live close to water
but never again by the sea
from which everything eventually

finds its way shore again—
arthritic driftwood, the bones
of dogfish and dogs, and Mr. Levi,
the wristwatch still on his wrist. Which is why
I believe the girl puts down the knife
and she rises, the river

                electric with light.

[ONE]

If I must choose a word,
let it be river

WE WILL BE LEFT AT GALILEE

I floated through this disordered life,
By chance I have managed to return alive.
—DU FU

I think it important to tell you

                that some will be barred from the journey.

I think it crucial to realize

              not everyone can go.
We will be forced to abandon our compasses
and our tattered maps,

             the faithful dog, blind and deaf, standing sentinel.
The nightlight left lit.

I think it imperative to go ahead and decide who
will hand out the pieces of paper,

who will pin the note explaining

              what took place
      to the sleeves.

These are the men I admit to leaving.
One, an actuary, knew exactly when people die.
One ushered in planes using
enormous orange flags. One kept his eyes
locked on mine when we kissed, quoted
Tang dynasty poems until I cried

stop, please, stop. One raced Italian bikes, *another day*
another second place, he laughed. One lived with four women
though not at the same time; loved, he said,
none of them. One knew only how to tickle me
until ecstasy.

     I admit there may be others.

Hey, Du Fu, going deeper and deeper between flowers, prepare me
a tonic
    to make my hair grow longer. Tell me
what will become of the poets?

Fanatics have their dreams,
         the savage too
guesses at heaven.

I think it important to acknowledge
         we're not all in this together.

I think it important to accept that not all the wounded
are going to pull through.

    Perhaps a few will understand when I say
lo mashireem ptzueem ba-shetakh
         doesn't always apply—
even to soldiers.

Yet this happened just yesterday—
I was stopped on the narrow highway leading
to the Sea of Galilee. Speed limit signs and stoplights
lined up like policemen on strike, all of them useless.
Traffic had backed up fifteen kilometers.
A few drivers leaned out of their vehicles, shading
their eyes, mouths twisted with the same bitterness
that clotted the August air, the smog
of the hundred idling engines. Slowly word worked back,
window to window, of a terrible accident. The girl
in the backseat looked up from the message
she was typing into her telephone,
there's no way around it, she said, her blue-green eyes
with the sun-lightened lashes meeting mine
in the mirror. Far ahead, smoke
began to rise and, one by one, the people stepped
from their cars and ran forward.

I think it crucial to confess that some
will beg to be taken

               though others will cover their mouths, cut
out their tongues.

I think it important to acknowledge that decisions
have already been made

and a few want to be left.

Even so,
           I think it essential to say to you
that we might not know
                    even at the end

if we've returned to Eden's outer reaches or again to the road,
to tell you
           what I've seen—
                    green and glintless
this driven-to
           this imaginary lake.

THIRD VERSION

The rain leaves fingerprints
in last summer's
window dust,

while just off shore, anchored
and waiting,
the barge that will ferry the lucky.

In one version of my story,
I sell my hair
and the good skin of my stomach.

In one version, I carry you
from the burning car
and this time you don't die.

The sea with the rubber hose of a river
down its throat
is swallowing as fast as it can.

If you watch long enough, you'll see that rain
shapes a path in the pane
for what falls behind it—

yet if you put a hand
to the glass,
the water will fall toward you.

Our lives are always half over.
There's still time.

HYMN

They exist
and I wake up to the thunk thunk
of tennis balls, the court at the country club already running,
the garbage trucks.
     I climb out of bed and they still exist.
The dog anxious to be let out, I wake up
to October clouds and sometimes there's rain.

This morning I turn on the news
to hear that physicists discovered a particle
immeasurably small they call
God that explains
     the difference between nothing
and rain, its granite mass.
They say they've seen it.

I get dressed in skinny jeans and pack an umbrella,
drive to the station, wait
for a train going south toward the city.
Every day I take a train
     and they still exist.
Outside the window
is a wall.
Outside the window are
     men, there are men
building a wall, men climbing
a wall. In Geneva

men built a machine to crash objects
traveling light speed
into each other, believing the particle
they call God
rubs off.
        They exist.
Outside the window there are new jails of white stone.
They exist outside the window.
                        They exist. On the train
a man strums a slow song
on guitar and sings in Russian. He stands
in front of me singing and I don't understand
and yet for a moment
he's singing
        of me.

CAPTAIN EVANGELIST

One must feel sorry
for atheists—they seem
so lonely.   All

by themselves, one
            among seven billion others astride
the endlessly recycling earth.

Turning to me
            in the airport bar,
the airplane captain said,
You won't know

how much   you need
God
      until you're sure
that you're dying.

After second glasses of Cabernet,
the captain told me,

If the seven billion refuse
to give you
what you really want,
                  you must teach yourself

not to want it.
            In the end,
you must teach yourself
to want

what you can get,

                he said, pressing my
hand against his face.

PILGRIM TO A VANISHING RIVER

The girls are the ones whose boyfriends went to war
without telling them, and their mothers see their own fates
in the coffee grounds going cold in the cup.

Their husbands left them too but not for war,
for more beautiful women.
The men never say goodbye.

I should tell you this: none of the pilgrims
are beautiful.

The men on the buses wear white shirts.
They are the last to leave the table because their daughters
will be ruined over and over.

They know that their souls will be reborn
in the bodies
                of small animals, and for this
they are grateful.
All the men grow thinner.

And I should tell you this: not one of the pilgrims
is the child of a senator.

They say, *we are grateful for what has befallen us.*
They are grateful
                for what has befallen them.

Three scientists—one Jew, one Muslim, and one Christian—
stand in the Jordan River.
They are trying to divide it into equal portions.

Each schemes to obtain more than his fair share.
They take samples of the water.
Meanwhile, unexploded munitions, hand grenades
and land mines float by.

The Jew sips the vial of water and says, *it tastes like Old Testament.*
The Muslim takes a drink, *no, more like Qur'an.*
The Christian says, *wait, wait, mine is turning into wine.*

The word "rival" is from the Latin *rivalis,* which describes competitors
for a river or stream. When I read this, my hands
begin shaking so hard I can scarcely turn the page.

This is a river that will never reach the sea.

At least not one that is living.

The three scientists come to the river
because the story they remember hearing as children
                        has grown quiet, emptied of everything
it once had to tell them.

When I drive up to the river to take a good look,
the three are standing knee deep
in its slow-moving filth.
                        They are looking down.

I stand on the bank and say, *God if you do exist—*
and it's then that I want to get down on my hands and knees
with the donkeys that aren't allowed to drink.

Many rivers have gone missing. I recognize this by the grief
they leave behind, the fossils of bony fish, imprints
of leaves.
                    A missing river is like a story of heroes

told over and over until it's true, at least as true
as the person telling it
as it was with Jesus, who arrived to the river a grown man.

And like heroes, a river
sometimes must be sacrificed, the animals too

that yearn to drink on its banks, dive
into the water. Also the pilgrims, the ugly women
and their ruined daughters, the men closing
                                        their eyes, slipping
beneath its surface.

ALL THE MIRACLES

Please St. Anthony, whether he's dead
or alive, whatever the outcome, please, let them
find him by nightfall, said a weeping woman

on Fox News. Five minutes later, my father
rang to tell me she was his best friend's daughter
whose three-year-old son had wandered

into the Louisiana swamps where they lived. *It didn't sound*
like her, my father said, but it was her name,
her face. St. Anthony, the patron of lost things.

For days, men and women, helicopters, dozens of dogs
scoured the wild, watery terrain near Bayou Teche.
When two found a sneaker by a pond,

they called in divers. After three days, I told my father,
the boy is dead. But that night,
a man armed only with a Bible and his best dog

spotted him asleep in the brush. *God led me*
straight to him, he told the cameras. Of miracles, my father
once said, they're like a path that leads out

from the grimmest war. My father, raised Catholic,
still talks about when the parish priest saw the Eucharist
become real flesh. The next day, WWII ended.

In today's paper, along with the Louisiana miracle,
someone else's child died in a fire; another boy
was accidentally shot in a drive-by. Reading over my shoulder,

the man next to me on the train said he'd once watched
a dead man come back to life. You should have seen
the doctor's face. *The look in his eyes, when he opened them.*

THE RUPTURE

There is another city
                    buried beneath this one.
With a hand I can touch it—
the sidewalk outside my house is embossed
with its print (just like the brocade dress of my dead mother
that I wear
                inside out and over it,
a thin woven coat of yellow cashmere and mull).

Once in Jerusalem, I looked into what I thought was a well,
saw a crowd pass beneath,
blondes and brunettes, the bald spots, tops of fedoras,
straw hats. The few faces raised,
                      those of small children, their eyes
unsurprised, the feral cats.

At the end of the last age, the great ice caps melted,
huge floods ripped the world's surface.
                      Beneath this city
are inhuman cities
assembled from ocean and calcium, constructed of shell, the remains
of boneless creatures
                like the light blue ones.
Still they drift blindly along the bottom.

How long can I be quiet?
When will the other city rise up, turn itself over? Pompeii, Atlantis
were erased from Earth's face
                in one day.

How long do I have
before the gods grow tired

                    living among the ruins?

THE AMERICAN IMPULSE

In Spielberg's famous film of *Close Encounters*,
the hero builds a mashed potato mountain
on his dinner plate, his mind's obsession—
a tower imagined.

He builds it again and again manically,
frantically, until the potatoes, a gray mess,

                                    won't hold on the table. His grip tight
on the knife,

he tells his children, their eyes
frightened holes, this means *something*. When asked
what he wants—*I just need to know*
                        it's happening.

It's not that we're innocent.
We know the cheating televangelist, now on his knees
and weeping, doesn't love his wife. We know the father in Kandahar
we rescued from bondage

will still trade his ten-year-old daughter
to an awful man thirty years older, and the daughter
will more likely die in childbirth than learn
to write her name.

And we know our hero, pursuing
that tower, will board the alien saucer leaving
his children fatherless.
                      He'll never look back.
It doesn't matter.

In the same way, we can't help
sending ourselves
            into the river, believing this time
we'll breach the place forbidden
to the untroubled. Singing all the way down,

    I am Orpheus; Oh this time, Eurydice, this time.

VERTIGO

in memory of Czesław Miłosz

The soul remembers that there is an up
and there is down. It recognizes the earth
and the trees, the breadth of a Negev desert.

The soul knows the delicate, the livable layer
between dirt and the vast blank expanse
of the universe. The soul draws the horizon.

The last time my mother and I climbed
the uneven steps up one of Jerusalem's
narrow alleys, she made a mistake

and looked down. She became so dizzy
she had to sit, and climb the remaining flight
on hands and knees. Not one

of the passersby offered to help. My mother
laughed, *perhaps they think I'm imagining
heaven's aerial stairs.* On her hands and her knees.

The soul trips over itself with each step,
the soul somersaults. But it's the soul that knows
it has to keep moving.

In a city somewhere, perhaps Paris or New York,
an émigré poet walks slowly along foreign streets.
In his arms, a microscope. Through it, he sees

that even on the tiniest scale *horror*
is the law of living things. The poet can't stop
looking through the eyepiece.

When vertigo first descended on my mother,
my father and I couldn't pretend otherwise. One day
she loved glass-paned elevators. The next day,

it was only if we huddled with her against the door.
She said, *it's like crossing a suspension bridge*
in a hurricane. She'd never been on a suspension bridge.

At the end, my mother sat in her chair
and barely moved, never looking down or turning her head.
She had trouble reading analog clocks.

The émigré poet writes poems about loss.
People in exile write many poems. He writes letters.
In one, he asks the Pope *what have they left to us*?

A wind rattles the windows of the house,
while outside, hundreds of red and gold leaves
rise up and up over an ice-skinned river.

This, though every tree I see is bare. My soul,
it is vertiginous. My soul shakes like dry sticks.
My soul, trembling,
                          an atom flung loose.

[TWO]

In the desert, there can be a mirage
of more than one river

NOTE EXPLAINING GOD TO CHILDREN

Our existence is a ripple on the surface of God is not what Spinoza said, but
it's what he meant. And for making such heretic waves, Amsterdam's rabbis
cursed him, expelling him from the Jewish fold in the same way Elisha con-
demned the jeering boys to the she-bear's claws and Joshua brought down
Jericho. They meant the Lord's sword would find him. Spinoza died a de-
cade later gagging on invisible slivers of glass inhaled while grinding lenses.
A death, one may say, from a thousand cuts.

So WHEN MY STEPDAUGHTER ASKED ABOUT GOD,
I TOLD HER:

God's a lot like gravity. He pulls things
toward each other. Though sometimes he throws them
into space with a slingshot and they're lost
forever. Then I told her, *God's a means
of measure* and like every number
has a unique place in a long list. And like God,

the numbers two and twelve don't exist
in space or time. But they exist.
A dozen eggs exist. Four yards
of fabric, two hundred barrels of oil. They'd exist
even if we didn't think of them that way.

Pythagoras discovered that the height of sound
is in inverse proportion to the length of string plucked
to make that sound. He bowed down
before the number and thought it

absolutely divine. *God is both abstraction and*
real being, I said, *the processor*
of all things.
                 She said, let's call him *Number One*.

It's not that I believe in afterlife. When I die, I believe I'll go back to the same place where I was born. I imagine my body becoming smaller and smaller, until the fetus devolves into the egg and sperm, then first the sperm, then the egg, wink out.

None of Pythagoras's writings survive.
Everything attributed to him comes to us
as hearsay, just as everything
attributed to God.

My best friend says God speaks with her in dreams, listens to her thoughts. She says that the cancer, which God knows about, is a test. She asks me to pray for her. Her older brother expects something even more devastating. He talks about tribulation, rains of fire, though is not specific of timing. He and his wife built a shelter and dug a well in the backyard of their Delaware mansion. They're installing generators, camouflaging propane tanks in the garden.

I was maid of honor at my friend's wedding. In the basement of the church where she married, there is a map showing the borders of Israel derived from writings in *Genesis* and *Ezekiel*. Israel, in this map, extends kilometers into Lebanon and Syria, and even makes inroads into Egypt. My friend has never tried to explain this map to me. This is how I know she loves me.

MESSAGE TO SPINOZA FROM ZBIGNIEW HERBERT:

> *God wants to be loved*
> *by the paranoid and cursed*
> *because they hunger*

Last week, my husband and I organized dinner for a businessman visiting Israel from Utah. He's Mormon. The Mormon felt compelled to tell us that *his kind* identifies with Jews because they too fled persecution. Later, when one of the Israelis told how his father helped settle Jews in Israel during the country's first years, the Mormon said, *your father must have been a Godly man.*

> *He was an atheist*, the Israeli replied.

MESSAGE FROM THE CHIEF RABBI OF ISRAEL WHEN ASKED TO LIFT SPINOZA'S CURSE AFTER FOUR HUNDRED YEARS:

> There's no Spinoza
> and God only knows how much
> there's no Spinoza

OTHER CHILDREN

[I]

Almost none of us were hurt
though the killers were children carrying rocks
for no reason except to close their small fists
around. Behind the limestone barricade,
we sipped wine of grapes grown in the Golan Heights
until the bottoms blackened,
but still the morning refused to come.

Still the children gathered.
On dirty placards they wrote,
Fanatics, as if we hadn't already noticed
the bandaged hands. How the youngest girl
kept removing
her socks and shoes. *It must be near
the end of it*, one woman said.
At dawn, another siren.

                We faced each other
while, in the grass,
the gray-hooded crows
for once were silent.

[II]

And the children go to school.
They scribble notes
to each other in the margins
of the one book they share.

The girl falls in love with her teacher.
The boy falls in love with the girl.
Neither learns
to read. The words in a language

that still hasn't been discovered.
The teacher recites
a form of mathematics—

                        that if ten things are wanted,
one will be had.

A VEIL

A baby's bulb glows, casting
a diffuse radiance
across an empty room.

                 Yet after so many years alone

in a Beijing orphanage, a Chinese child
will say that all white faces
forever *look the same*,
never having seen one.

                 And just like that,

a human bond forms
from a silent dialogue

                 between naked faces, weaves
its fragile cloth.

After a stroke, my mother's friend,
just fifty years old, lost the ability

                 to discern her sons' faces
from any others.

Even if we show her their photos again
and again. Every day she wakes trembling
to strange children.

So when I say,

           take off the veil
and face me

               it's because I need more than eyes,

more than the slit
of your amber iris. When I look

in Rembrandt's portraits, there seems to me
a promise
that a great many faces will be lost—

Aristotle and a Bust of Homer, Bathsheba
at Her Bath, The Man
in a Gold Hat—and lost

                more than once,

but he'll have no hand in it.
How could any of us

          bear ourselves,
the beloved's face
painted over?

AFGHANI ROMANTICS

In Kabul, there are drug addicts young
as a month. When the sirens sound,
their mothers calm them
with lullabies, gently blowing

opium smoke in their mouths. In Kabul,
fathers and granddaughters share
the single needle. In Kabul, they like to say
Americans are also infected—

by cashmere, so that its men develop
fevered rashes and twitch if forced
to sleep in anything
but silk. *Komfortismus*, they call it,

that dread burger-state
of dull emasculation where below the belt,
a smell of fetid wreckage. Inside Kabul's
most famous opium den,

a Taliban fighter delivers a vial
to the woman with the whitest skin, blue veins
spidered along her wrists. The only skin
visible. The fighter whispers

as she takes it, *those men
will eventually leave because they need Pepsi Cola
and Egyptian cotton sheets*. His index finger
on her sleeve, he says, *we need only this.*

LETTER TO FLAUBERT

Dear Gustave,

       You wrote that you saw Byron's name
written on one of the pillars in the dungeon
where the Prisoner of Chillon
was confined. Since then, I'm thinking more
about Byron than the prisoner, whose brothers
starved there beside him, one after another.
No images come to me of torture
or slavery. For weeks, I've been thinking only
of the pale man who one day went there,
walked up and down, his club foot
carving a line in the dust, traced his name
on the stone, and left. The idea
of Byron's name, I tell you, fills me
with fear. A man would have to be
very foolish to write his name in such a place.

Yet Gustave,

       there has to be something
beyond the given.

It's not that if Byron had been born
in another country, if he'd had boy children,
he might have strapped bombs
to their bodies. Sent them into the churches.
It's not that if kitchen tables aren't given,
then kitchen tables can become
catfish, catfish become factory managers, factory

managers become hammers.
It's not that there are those
who say Muhammad
was a fiery mass of Life cast up
from the great bosom of Nature. That Jesus also.
It's not just that Byron abandoned
the people who loved him, over and over.

Gustave,

      Byron wrote that when cut free, the Prisoner
of Chillon yearned only for return
to his manacled martyrdom, his miserable cell.
Don't believe it.
               I've seen him running,
shouting a name
            into the unfettered air.

A MAN'S HAND

It's mid-April, the Mediterranean breeze
        already filled with June heat. I've hours
of climbing to go. On morning TV—

the news that Ashraf Meriyah, an Israeli soldier
        from the Druze village Daliat el-Carmel
where I just bought supplies for my hike, shot

himself in the head. It was before dusk. He was alone
        on leave in the small room he shared
with his younger brother. I imagine the taste of metal,

how his hands must have reached out
        for his rifle's trigger. Underfoot, lichen
black as soot slickens the limestone path rising

above a still spring-green Jezreel Valley. In my bag,
        pita spread thick with labaneh cheese, baklava,
just baked, the smell almost too sweet in the warm air.

By now I should have reached *Mukhraka*,
        the burned place, where Elijah mocked
the worshippers of Baal by lighting a stone pyre

with just water, and then murdered Baal's
        four hundred and fifty prophets. On hearing
of his suicide, Ashraf's best friend

Louis Nasser a-Din, still on base, also shot
         himself in the head. No one in Daliat el-Carmel
mentioned either of their sons. I didn't ask. After Elijah

slaughtered Baal's prophets, his servant saw
         an enormous cloud form into a man's hand
signaling, Elijah says, God's pleasure.

NOTE FROM THE LEDGE

Someone shot through the chest feels pain
just the second it takes the bullet
to pierce those three inches of breast
and bone. The second it takes to stop
the heart's beating. That doesn't sound
like long, but consider the ache
of anticipation,

                of the waiting.

When I talk about waiting, it's not
about hostages, gun barrels
pressed to their heads. Every hostage believes
he'll be saved. I'm talking about the man
in front of a firing squad.
I'm asking you:

                who's going to rescue him?

No one rescued DB (DB is not his *real* name),
an Israeli businessman known
for his investment savvy.
DB leapt from the 17th-story window of his office
in the same building as my husband's.

For months before he jumped,
he kept telling his wife, his four children, even
strangers in elevators:

                I am already dead.
How is it you see me?
He asked his four-year-old son,

                are you a ghost?

What does he feel as he falls
those last two hundred feet, the familiar
faces at windows, the grasping
of air. That there's no ending, only in the idea
of an ending? His eyes set
to the second hand
of his watch. Most people who jump
from bridges and tall buildings
don't scream.

            Though some do.

A few days later, I tell my husband
that Utah executed a man by firing squad.
His only comment:

         why does the world call Israel barbaric?
What does Utah have to do with Israel? I ask.

After dinner and a not-quite-chilled Chardonnay,
my husband says, *when DB was standing*
on the ledge,
someone below yelled, "jump, jump, jump!"

You're right, he says, pouring
more wine into our glasses,

         we're all barbarians.

All night, I hear people screaming
 as they tumble

        toward death, a chorus

of onlookers urging them on. If they could,
would those suicides, mouths
wide open,
        claw their way back
through the open windows?

There's only one major US bridge
from which no one's leapt—Utah's East Canyon Dam.
Perhaps a few intend to,
but it's a long drive to get there.
After hours by themselves
in their Ford Fiestas, their Volkswagen Cabriolets,
they change their minds.

See them in their cars, screaming their heads off.

POSTCARDS FROM GETHSEMANE

[I] Church of the Holy Sepulchre

It seems I've hardly arrived
And another year has gone by.
I send you this picture postcard:
May the year and its curses end
And may my river one day run full.
May the unbelievable stop me when it strikes,
As does the bowl of wonder.
I should tell you that every dawn still there is Venus,
Until little by little at the start,
Larger and larger it advances.
The red bowl of my redemption.
I refuse to condition it.
Soon I will be older.
Soon I will have accumulated enough time.
So that when I wake in the morning,
I will undress.
I will be as Samson, his tresses grown back.
That which has been is that which shall be.
Until when? Until when? you ask.
Perhaps when another year has gone by.

[II] CENTRAL TRAIN STATION

                    It's years later. There's still no sign
of an End. The entire affair
has to be buried. Along
with those ugly angels in their ultramarine
frocks. *Ascend toward God, send word*
of our divine master, someone joked
to the priest. Perhaps something went wrong
at the railroad station. God forgot
to change trains or accidentally
killed the conductor. All the passengers
have vanished. The criminals
have outlived their children and the saints,
they've gone home too.
I will be understood less and less,
but a wind, the priest once said, *is blowing*
in my favor. It's years later. There's no sign
of an End. For the mayor,
it's a scandal. For the innkeeper,
someone's hair's in the salad. I'm afraid
there is no other paradise. This
must be it.

[III] In the Garden of Gethsemane

And so it will happen, my Love,
When the gift of light isn't thrown away
When it drops its full weight on us
When the dog at last found could be our own
When madness will be the insistence he's not
When the steel splint supporting the mythic olive tree finally snaps
When Gethsemane's statues are no longer taken for granted
When the risk is to remain locked in the ground
When the agony is more than it takes to grow out of it
When between holm oak wood and box-tree hedge, a bower
When the three marble men reach out their arms
When they pull back their bows
When madness will be the insistence they're nothing but stone
When the revelation is our silence.

GHAZAL AT THE END

When will prophets be praised? At the end?
Martyrs expect to be paid at the end.

But what of the dark-haired girl hidden
from the father. Who's more crazed at the end?

The lip, the wrist, the hollow of her neck
the *YesYesYes*, her dress raised at the end.

Afterward when I told you I loved someone
else, you screamed you were betrayed at the end.

Jesus—like any flawed man—from the cross:
why have you forsaken me at the end.

No cup, no fountain, no extinct flower
with white stamen. Yet more days at the end.

With me on my knees, my mouth and my head
in his hands. How his eyes blazed at the end.

Blind old woman of Thebes, were you a secret
pagan, or a true saint at the end?

The footprint. The fort. The moat unable to hold
water. Even when erased at the end.

Sarah, my mother once said, *there are no heroes, no*
saints, and,   *no princess waits to be saved.*
        at the end,

[THREE]

*Down one river, there is a ruined house, down
another, empty boats bobbing*

AFTER THE LONG PILGRIMAGE

The old pilgrim says, taking my hand, *prophecies*
have one thing in common:
each reveals itself as just another workday.

Morning.
              Then the smell of coffee.
A clink of cutlery.

In any case, afterwards, there is for a time
no ghost in the closet,
at least until the dogs wake and begin their howling.

During the rebellion against Rome, he says, *the Jews*
burned the last sheaves of wheat, poured
all the water on the ground, entirely placing their fate
in God's hands.   They forced Him to act.

It's the day after the last day,
he says,
        that's always
the most dangerous.

THE PUZZLE

A strange fog has settled
in the yard, clouds fallen straight
down. Their cloth weight. My face soaked
in water. In the basement
my stepdaughter is playing
with a friend. They've turned over
an old box of blocks and toy
parts, they've spread out all the small
dusty pieces. The girls toss
them one by one back into
the container. From below
I hear whispers. *Pretend we're*
sisters. Pretend our mother
has been killed, our father turned
into a monster. Slowly
their hushed voices move upstairs
to enter the kitchen. *Look*
what we found, they say, their hands
and pockets full of tiny
cardboard puzzle pieces. They
carefully set them down in
the center of the kitchen
table. *Pretend we're sisters,*
pretend our father's been put
under a spell by a witch,
our mother is dead. The girls
ask me to cut up apples,
if I'll open a carton
of chocolate milk. Drops of mist

condense, run down the window's
edges. I can't remember
how to tell her, it's almost
time for dinner. How to say,
careful, darling girl, some spells
aren't supposed to be broken.

THE BURN UNIT

In the burn unit of the old city hospital
there are two kinds of people—

                            dreamers

and those who don't.

Those who don't dream

                            move delicately,

even the ones who still have
their eyelashes. They try not to blink or stumble,

understanding that one small bump
against a gurney, the leg
of a table, and they'll need more than morphine.

So they're never too close to the furniture
or to each other. They consider
even a soft cloth

                            a threat.

The dreamers are also frightened
of handling. In the lounge they've code-named
Anesthesia, there are whispers—

of burning bushes, eight-headed
beasts with sixteen wings, discussions
of which antidotes to mix as precaution.

Some nights, the youngest dreamer
tiptoes down the burn unit hall, quiet
except for a hum of machinery, calling out,

Olly Olly In Come Free.

All of them—
               dreamers and those who don't—hide
in the stairwells and supply closets. No one
wants to wake up.

NIGHT HOUSES

[I]

Last night, I moved into your house. Oh how this quickened the pulse. It stopped me from sleeping (or maybe it's what kept rousing me). It was a night metamorphosed into day. Your house, cedar shingled and shuttered, clung with fingernails to a steep granite cliff. From a broken window and through a band of wind-beaten cypress, an ocean threw itself upon a pebbly shore, while far south, rested the skeleton of a skiff. Last night, even afterwards, I remembered the ocean's name, but not your face.

Your house was falling apart. There was the clogged plumbing, an infestation of black mold, all the bannisters loose. The basement flooded with even the smallest of rains. Your house was still uncharted. Cubbyholes and crooked hallways opened to balconies, terraces, to unexpected walls and dead ends. Some rooms had regular shapes, rectangular, while others rounded or sloped with oddly degreed corners. A low-ceilinged attic hovered, a small portal opening east. Squirrels kept finding their way in. There were places to hide and locked doors whose keys had gone missing.

To think of an empty house is *impossible*.

[II]

Behind the house where I live now, another
is going up. It has three floors, a concrete staircase
still without rails, gray bones visible
through enormous windows that seem
like eyes peering out
over a raw plot where one day might be a garden—

what blooms, changes, falls to ruin, awakens, what leaves.

Today, a neighbor tells me the young couple
building the house separated
after the husband's lover sent his wife pictures.
I'd wondered for weeks.

Why some nights, a small white light moves
window to enormous window, the house
half-finished and empty, except
for someone, like me,

                who isn't sleeping.

A WINDOW IS TO REACH THROUGH

He's stood like that, an hour or more,
one hand holding open
the window's curtain. In that time,

it's turned dusk to dark
                                    so that the white
undershirt, the shade of face, the close cropped head

turn opaque. The bedside lamp behind cuts
out his shape from the light.
                                    For more than an hour

he's stared toward me where I sit
at my own window, wondering if he's going to
step through.

                I want to believe
that it's at me
he won't stop looking and I'm happy

to be here in this darkened room
holding a book of stories by Chekhov.
Everyone I know is lonely
                                    even though we say
we're here for each other.

From the road, I hear an ambulance
taking one of the elderly from a nearby house.
I turn on a light

so the book in my hand swims
                              back into focus,
the phone rings
and then again is quiet.

THE KEY

It's impossible for me to throw
away a key.
        Though I've tried
153 times just this week. That's how many keys hang
in one of my cupboards on five rows
of five hooks each. The keys came with the house
my husband and I bought three months ago
from a retired couple who lived there
their entire married lives.

Assyrians, or it might have been the ancient Greeks,
invented lock and key

first out of wood, then made of metal. Before that,
cords of rope made of rush and fiber
                                fixed doors, bound
the criminals. Back then, it was the knot
that let people in
               and kept them out.

When Gordius, King of Phrygia,
wanted to secure his seat to the shaft of his chariot
so that no one could steal it,
he tied so intricate a knot that *the man who could untie it*
would conquer all of Asia.
                  So the legend went.
But when Alexander the Great failed
to undo it with just his fingertips, he sliced
the Gordian Knot clean through with a sword.

There are twenty-one doors inside our house,
all with locks, their keys always
in them.
               We've also two safes, one set
in concrete by the first couple, one installed by us
when we couldn't open theirs.

On my twenty-five hooks, there are keys
for cars built forty years ago, keys
for padlocks and old fashioned boxes.
There are seven
                         gold skeleton keys
with long cylindrical shafts, carved
rectangular teeth. One such key has an ornate handle
in the shape of a half-open flower.

I keep keys to every door I've ever closed,
every house left.
               Now I have 153 more for which,
in this whole house, I can't find
a single matched lock, 153 keys that don't fit
any of our doors or safeguard anything.
My husband asks,
               why keep them? I ask,
how could they leave them behind?

NOTE ON DADAISM

I cross a small meadow to the installation, a low beige concrete bunker held off the ground by four squat legs. A small hatch underneath releases easily and warily I raise my head through the opening. Dry leaves blow from one side of the gray interior to the other, gathering in small piles.

Dreams remind us
of what we want, dreams remind us
we want to want.
You say that perhaps the dream
is telling me
not to be afraid.
Then I remember that it isn't dreams
that remind us of what we want,
but our memories.
But it's true. I don't want
                         to be afraid.

One side of the installation is open to the outside but covered by a wire mesh screen. The screen allows small animals, mice, moles, to enter for protection but prevents the larger from following. Through the mesh, I watch a raccoon chase a ball through the grass. Such joy. Then I see the ball is a tiny rabbit. I become frightened. The rabbit disappears. In his place, a small clump of cacti.

Why do the men I love
                         never appear in my dreams?

On this day in 1914, James Joyce published *Dubliners*. It had taken nine years. Joyce said he merely wished to give the Irish "one good look at themselves in my nicely polished looking-glass," that it wasn't his fault "that the odour of ashpits and old weeds and offal hangs round my stories." I still remember the last lines of Joyce's story "Eveline" as she, in the end, refuses to follow her lover onto the ship and away from her terrible life, "She set her white face to him, passive, like a helpless animal. Her eyes gave him no sign of love or farewell or recognition."

My life, really, is not terrible.

Do you remember our trip to the Israeli artist's village Ein Hod? Marcel Janco, a Romanian Dadaist, founded the colony in the late 1940s. Janco immigrated to Palestine during WWII, realizing Dadaism was done and Eastern Europe no safe place for aging Dadaist Jews. Janco's painters, sculptors, and writers moved in after its Arab occupants "abandoned" the village during the Arab-Israeli War that followed. The Arabs left behind their tables, chairs, blankets, leaving even the fat candles in their metal holders. Later, some of the Arab residents returned to the village, but they never got their homes or their fat candles back.

How does one achieve
eternal bliss? By saying dada.
                               How does one
become famous? By saying dada.
With a noble gesture and delicate
propriety. Till one goes crazy.
                             Till one loses consciousness.

There was only one issue of the Dadaist journal *Cabaret Voltaire* ever published.

I didn't buy anything in the artist's village
except for a cerulean ceramic vase, the artist's name
inscribed on its base. I think it looks best filled
with plastic red Gerbera daisies and

                              nailed to the wall.

RACK OF LAMB

A pistachio tree straightens
toward the light. The light embracing
its leaves. Dumb tree. Dumb flaming orb.
I name each one of them, my own.

Pour of cardamom tea, the slow
shuff of low tide like an echo
of a lover's breath, a casting
out of birds' nests,

                 all those laced nests
gathering in gutters, and the warm rain
that chases them. Say my name back
at me. Dumb you. Dumb human heart.

I am preparing rack of lamb
with crushed pistachio. I cry
over the dead lamb, shorn of wool,
the pink meat, over its tiny
broken ribs.

            My husband's mother
prepared the same dish. Years from now,
my husband will tell me he never
liked lamb, even his mother's.

Let this happen with no *khamsin*,

                       in a year with no hot desert
coat of *sharav*, in the year when
Israel's grape yield isn't halved,
eaten by chukar partridges
feasting on the low-hanging fruit.

There are more than seven hundred
pistachio trees growing wild
in Israel's remotest deserts;
some are centuries old—their fruit
inedible.
       All those wasted
lambs, all that inaudible light.

MERCY

I believe in sin, or at least I believe in it
as much as I do in divinity
and perhaps a little more than I believe

the world will end next Wednesday,
which was the message hand-printed in black
on both sides of a sign held high by a man,

his face hungrily thin, at the east entrance
to Tel Aviv's central train station. Through the white
he'd washed over the cardboard, I could make out

the words: /THIS SIDE UP/. He stood there
all day. I passed him on the way in
to catch a morning train, the way out ten hours later.

Nietzsche wrote that weak men invent gods
because they need to punish themselves for not being born
powerful. They invent horror stories

so they can explain their scars.
The man spoke to me as I walked by. He said,
the day of rapture is the end of God's mercy.

I believe in sin. I believe in it almost as much
as I do, for instance, in Charles Dickens though a hell
of a lot more, I admit, than I believe

his story of Oliver Twist, who never once
in Dickens's novel held back a quid for himself.
No starving boy should ever be that virtuous.

As for Nietzsche, he suffered a mental collapse
only three years after publishing his theory
dissecting weaklings and gods. They say his last act

was to throw himself weeping between
a worn-out horse and its owner who was beating it
to death. What I really believe is no one

       is perpetually punished.

ANOTHER YEAR OF SIN

I would like to entrust my sins to the waters,
let them be carried to the sea.
— CZESLAW MILOSZ, *Rivers*

At dusk, the world goes quiet—
of cars and buses, motorbikes and sirens. The television
programming blinks off, lawnmowers and leaf blowers
haphazardly stowed. The highways
empty out. Slowly the roads refill
with children on bicycles, skaters and skateboarders, their excited dogs
loping leashless alongside, while on dusty benches
and dirty curbs, their parents recline to chat
with neighbors, whom they realize suddenly
they haven't seen in months. In Israel,
if you die on Yom Kippur,
you have to wait.

Yesterday, walking our small brown and white spaniel
through Park Se'adya Shoshani, my husband and I watched
a religious Jew dressed in black hat and coat wave
what looked from a distance
a feathered boa
over the head of a small boy
who could not have been more
than three. Closer, I realized the boa was in fact
a live white chicken. *The chicken soaks up*
the past year's sins, my husband said, looking
a bit embarrassed. The white chickens
are then slaughtered, so that the year's evil
dies with them.

I'll send photos tomorrow of Ayalon Highway, clean
except for pedestrians and bicyclists
to a friend in New York, who doesn't believe
that no one, I mean no one, drives
the whole day of Yom Kippur. For one day, in Israel,
there is nowhere to drive. Tomorrow
I'll call her. I know she'll think hilarious
the story of the white chicken, the Orthodox boy, who himself
couldn't stop laughing, trying to grab
the flapping white bird from his father. Anyway,
in a few hours, the Israelis
will get back in their cars, but right now I hear
the Yarkon River, half a kilometer away, the weight
of the past year being cast off.

SAYING JERUSALEM

It's become tricky to talk about Jerusalem
these days. Tricky, that is, without saying
cinnamon trees and *narrow alleys, overfed
sparrows*, or *Hasidic boys in metal spectacles*.

I've nothing to say about trees or sparrows
or quaint Jerusalem characters, mustached men
selling talismans. *Why don't you like Arabs,*
one asked, when I tried to bargain. Some Israelis joke

all we really need is Tel Aviv and the freeway
to Ben Gurion airport. Let the Arabs and fanatics
fight over everything else. From the roof
of my Tel Aviv house, I can sometimes glimpse

Jerusalem, the gleaming tip of al-Haram ash-Sharif.
Let them have everything else. Everything.

WHAT THE KESTREL CALLS THE CANYON

In a picture taken from space, the Makhtesh
appears to me like an eye. Not half open and staring
but an eye's veiny back as it peers down
and into Israel's Negev desert. A baseball-capped Brit
sharing a bench with me on the Makhtesh overlook says
the harsh mountainous expanse reminds him
of America's Grand Canyon. A blonde woman,
I suppose his wife, says it's like an ocean trench
that's too deep for any significant life. I shake my head.
Not a canyon. Not trench.
Those are opened by earthquake or volcanic
explosion, excavated through the erosion
of centuries-running rivers. Literally, Makhtesh means
stone bowl. I tell them, there's just no good word
for it in English. At this great jagged hole

there used to be a single mountain whose granite tip
slipped off over the slow course
of two hundred million summers. Exposed,
the soft sandstone interior was spooned out
by winds from Egypt, pounded down
by rain's pestle. In Melville's *Moby-Dick*, Captain Ahab nails
a doubloon to his ship's mast, and in the coin's pagan symbols
every shipmate envisions something different. Starbuck sees
a heartless God, Stubb man's life as an eternal cycle, Flask
pictures the gold's worth only in dollars and handfuls
of rolled cigars. Which reminds me of what Sigmund Freud
supposedly said—sometimes a cigar is just a cigar.
Melville would have said, it never is. By jeep

it takes my husband and me four hours to traverse just part
of the Makhtesh's twenty kilometer span. Inside

the jagged mineral depths, I collect
the fossilized shells of small animals interned
in what used to be an enormous sea, rocks rippled
with greenish copper, striped
with purple quartz. Two thousand years ago,
Nabatean Arab cameled caravans crossed
the Makhtesh every few months ferrying frankincense
and red pepper from Yemen through Petran cities
and finally to Gazan ports. It took those early Arabs
sixty-seven days and more water than they could carry.
Every fifty kilometers, they dug another well, built
another fortress. Now, a few tumbled stones
are all that remains of their long-abandoned towns.

My husband calls the Makhtesh, *be-risheet*
meaning *in the beginning*, which is the Hebrew name
of the Torah's first book. He points out
that this close to sea level, clean water lies
only a few centimeters beneath the Makhtesh's
arid surface. Listening to him, I kneel beside a ravine, knotweed
and thistle green, suddenly spotting tens
of shallow wells burrowed by thirsty hyraxes
and the shy desert rats. Looking up, I want to tell him
Makhtesh might just as easily mean *in the end*
as above us, a yellow-necked kestrel slowly circles
searching the wells' drying edges
                                        for signs of his dinner.

BIRDS OF THE OLD CITY

The Arab waiter skirts the courtyard's
circular fountain, discreetly pulling
bits of broken bread
from his pocket for the birds, two
doves dropping down
from the bows of a young tree,
the sparrows watching.

They don't forget, he says,
glancing at the branch swaying
under their weight,
the old custom to catch small birds,
skin, roast, and sell them
two sparrows for a penny.
                              One bird
to a mouthful.

[FOUR]

My worship of rivers
is a worship of what flows

NEAR DEATH EXPERIENCE

This might be heaven.
                              Above, someone is holding
hands with an astronaut, light years
among the space junk (exploded satellites and bits
of spent rockets, wrenches dropped
by the space-walkers). Schoolchildren track
the debris cloud from earth.

                              The risen say that their souls
fly to the ceiling where they see, for the first time,
their own beauty. I don't believe they leave their bodies
so much as travel to a place where
they can be rescued.
                    Don't they all come back?
And the astronaut who wakes from gravity's dream,
he too cries out.
              To know finally
that all astronauts must die.

In his dream, the astronaut shows his daughter
                                        how water
stays pressed against the bottom of an orbiting pail.
Until his arm tires. Then he opens his eyes
just in time
              to fire his ship's thrusters—break free
from what we used to call heaven.

WHALE FALL

Beneath this fragile ship, brittle stars
and snow crabs gather
in the whale's carcass, hagfish and deep sea sleeper sharks
nibble on the decomposing body
leaving only tatters
for the sea scuds, the slower moving lobster,

which is an odd way to summon resurrection,
how there exist wormlike creatures that return to life
only in a fallen whale, their dormant selves drifting
mindless miles beneath the ocean's surface
until they chance across another body
and only there, flourish,

until it's finished, and then they perish,
sending out again
                    their unconscious vessels.

A MIRAGE OF SHORE

Every twenty meters along a beach, the same sign—
a stick figure drawn in red, arms raised
above stick figure red waves.
The international sign for dangerous waters.

Even so, the sea is filled with bobbing heads, their hair
slickened to the same shade.

From fifty meters out, the shore becomes another horizon.

In summer, a fine sand coats the old leaves,
the wilting flowers, and the cars, newly cleaned,
the blue tiled table resting
in our Tel Aviv garden. I've quit fighting.

I keep the windows closed tight during
the worst, tilt the chairs into the table so the dust
won't settle. The view through a window screen
slowly turns brown. Then winter. Then a month of rain.

This far out, the shore seems an illusion.

All around me is the sea. No, not the sea, it's a garden
of blue bottles, shattering, then growing
solid, as if by a glassblower's mouth, then again
shattering. And through them, my pale arms. No, a phantom
of pale arms, in the glass, hovering, which turns
the bottles see-through then to stone.

From this far, the shore a mirage—

I wave wildly at my husband, standing in the surf,
his daughter's red hair like a marigold.

—the shore I am swimming for and the shore.

When I stumble from the water, I realize
I've drifted half a kilometer south, the man and the child
I'd been waving at, strangers. From up the beach, I see
a figure running, shouting my name.

REPRISAL

It's in the same grasp of the chalice,

                                    the last sigh

of the knight's desire,
his annihilation.

                    Oh, I went to the sea.

I splashed at the surf's edges,
my clumsy hands grabbing
for the sand

            as it ran back

toward the water. But it wasn't what I wanted—

I just couldn't admit the tide's perfect
futility. That asleep beneath the rotting ship
as it disintegrates, the storied knight
who finally wins the golden fleece

must be killed instantly.

                      Or he lives

weakened by what he wants to love
and nowhere to pursue it.

AT THE BORDER

There in the white field, I will rise
from the row I am furrowing with such ardor
and begin walking. I will walk again

                        to the edge

of the actual river

as so often I have walked to its edge.

I will get up this time slowly
and walk to the river—

beloved to me
                in its everpresentness.

How many children do you have?

I had one, a water ghost, a see-through
creature, nocturnal, a night lover. When born, she dissolved
through my fingers.

Which is to say I have none.

A boy once told me: *I like you
                as much as a tadpole;
maybe one day, it'll become a frog.*

Even tadpoles scream underwater, I said back,
which is true, but superfluous.

Do you have any family here?

No, lucky for them.

How long are you staying?

That's not the right question.

How long are you staying?

I've stayed already too long.

                    And so on.

I go back to that drunken evening
when I took a young man I'd known less than four hours
to The Hotel Pierre. We made love
in garbled voices and in
the bones of his hips and my knees
and his teeth and mine.

Afterwards,

            What was that? I asked and he,
What was *that?*

When he turned on the light
we saw that we were both painted

in our wetness, in my blood.
I hadn't realized my period was near
or perhaps I thought I'd willed it
away. I could see the print of my hand
on his arm, his face
and underneath his fingernails
the red of me.

He started laughing, saying first in Italian
then English, *someone*
was born, or died I wanted to add.
He led me from that bed
to the shower and we washed
each other clean.

We spent two more messy nights
together.
              And then I left.

I was still married and the boy,
he was too young for me.
Real concerns, yes,
                    but more
I was afraid of becoming ridiculous.

I left his messages
unanswered.
              And so on.

I've tried shooting them
one by one
          like small flightless birds
                in an open field,
raking them
like last year's leaves.

Still, regrets
        return
in an endless arcade game.
                A shadow
passing over my bedclothes,

the unseen bird over water.

In the dream of the white field, I rise
and shed my dress,
I shed my hair and my skin, I leave

        my arms and both knees
at the edge.

I, who lived
a long time in one place,
           am Daphne released

from her Laurel prison of
leaves and roots. She, who lived

                    a long time in one place.

I slide down to the actual river, its bank
blurred
        with feather grass and reeds.
                    I want to say

I threw myself in. Its current
was strong.
               I want to say
that this time
        I let it take me.

REVISING PROPHESY

I stood once in one of Rome's churches
and I watched
                what seemed tears
seep from the stone eyes
of St. Teresa.

I saw her lips part.
                   But if I say *pain*,
I've stolen a word from the mouth
of a saint. And if I say *grief,* what of Teresa's frenzy,
the stopped-forever small death, and the way

her robes seem to want to fall open?
                      If I say *faith*,
what of her flesh? It wasn't just from faith
Bernini sculpted that form.

                      Once outside Buchenwald's gates,
I thought I heard Robert Desnos
reading the palms of his death row inmates, foretelling
long lives, the men's return

to small chairs by open windows.
But if I say *prophesy*, I've pilfered the hope
from his poetry,
the headlong pursuit toward that open window

even though annihilation
was its only real end. And if I say *truth*,

what of Desnos, his shaved head bent
over paws of men

who would not stop stepping forward,
the tenderness with which he traced
                                    their futures?
What finally of *his* fall?

And when I tell you, *I believed*
I would love you forever;
                        I'm only saying
we're not fools.

There is delicious disorder
to the orbits of planets and stars
                        and three or four years from now
it may be spring again.

Your daughters will gather
stones, their voices sneaking up on you
high pitched in girlish glee: *die, die, die,*
which in their language means nothing more
than *stop it.*

And if on that day you stand alone
on your balcony
looking west all the way

to the Mediterranean Sea, don't think
this too will pass.

The Jacaranda tree will explode
to blue, branches weighted
with flocks of evening birds,
the Judas tree will again wear roped robes
of red and white flowers.

We'll no longer be together.
I make no other claim for you
except to say, *it's only one more horizon.*
It's not the end
                  of anything.

NOTES

["We Will Be Left at Galilee."]
The phrase, "lo mashireem ptzueem ba-shetakh," which is a transliteration of Hebrew, is the equivalent of the military motto in English, "leave no man behind."

["Pilgrim to the Vanishing River."]
The river mentioned is the Jordan River, a 250-kilometer-long river rising from Jordan, Lebanon, and Israel and flowing to the Dead Sea. The Jordan River serves as a water source for Lebanon, Jordan, Israel, Syria, and the West Bank area of the Palestinian Territories. In Christian tradition, Jesus was baptized in it by John the Baptist.

["The American Impulse."]
The movie referenced is *Close Encounters of the Third Kind*, written and directed by Steven Spielberg and released in 1977.

["Notes Explaining God to Israeli Children."]
Baruch Spinoza (1632–1677) was a Jewish Dutch philosopher who developed highly controversial ideas regarding the authenticity of the Hebrew Bible and the nature of the Divine. Many consider Spinoza one of the great rationalists of the seventeeth century; many also consider him an atheist. The Amsterdam Rabbinate issued a Cherem (excommunication) against him when he was twenty-three. Spinoza lived quietly as a lens grinder until his death.

["Letter to Flaubert."]
The Château de Chillon (Chillon Castle) is located on the shore of Lake Geneva, three kilometers from Montreux, Switzerland. In 1816, Lord Byron and Percy Bysshe Shelley visited the castle. Byron was inspired to write

a sonnet and, later, a 392-line narrative poem chronicling the imprisonment of a Genevois monk, Francois Bonivard, from 1532 to 1536 in the castle's dungeon. Much of the first stanza of my poem is inspired by a letter Gustave Flaubert wrote to Alfred Le Poitteven dated May 26, 1845, which described Flaubert's visit to this same castle.

["A Man's Hand."]
The story of the prophet Elijah comes from the Christian Old Testament (Hebrew Bible) 1 Kings Chapter 18.

["Night Houses."]
The line "To think of an empty house is *impossible*" comes after imperfectly reading Gaston Bachelard's *The Poetics of Space*. In it, he writes, "Maybe it is a good thing for us to keep a few dreams of a house that we shall live in later, always later, so much later, in fact, that we shall not have time to achieve it. For a house that was final, one that stood in symmetrical relation to the house we were born in, would lead to thoughts—serious, sad thoughts—and not to dreams. It is better to live in a state of impermanence than in one of finality."

["A Window Is to Reach Through."]
After Eamon Grennan's poem "Woman at Lit Window."

["Rack of Lamb."]
In Israel, *sharav* or *khamsin*, is a hot, dry, desert wind that blows from the Arabian Desert from May to mid-June and from September to October. It typically lasts for two to five days at a time.

BIOGRAPHICAL NOTE

Sarah Wetzel is also the author of *Bathsheba Transatlantic*, which won the Philip Levine Prize for Poetry and was published in 2010. After job-hopping across Europe and the Americas, Sarah currently teaches creative writing at The American University of Rome, dividing time between Manhattan, Rome, and Tel Aviv. Sarah holds an engineering degree from Georgia Tech and an MBA from Berkeley. More importantly for her poetry, Sarah completed an MFA in Creative Writing at Bennington College in January 2009. You can read more of her work at www.sarahwetzel.com.